MY BLUEPRINT FOR SUCCESS

A NOVICE'S GUIDE TO STEPPING ONTO THE PATH OF NETWORK MARKETING MASTERY

THE BASICS FOR BEGINNERS

FLOYD J. SANDERS

Table of Contents

Introduction to Network Marketing

Welcome, intrepid explorers, to the captivating realm of network marketing, where ambition ignites, and dreams take flight. In this dynamic field, entrepreneurial spirits converge with the power of personal connections, creating a unique ecosystem that defies the boundaries of traditional business models. Network marketing, often referred to as multi-level marketing (MLM), stands as a beacon of opportunity, beckoning those who seek a non-conventional path to success.

Picture yourself at the helm of your own enterprise, where your business acumen, eloquence, and unwavering determination intertwine to forge a path toward financial independence and personal growth. Network marketing is not merely about accumulating wealth; it's a journey of self-discovery, community building, and realizing one's untapped potential beyond the confines of a monotonous 9-to-5 routine.

If you yearn to shape your destiny and embark on a career that values genuine relationships and relentless effort, network marketing may very well be the gateway to your dreams. It's a realm where your business acumen, communication skills, and determination intertwine to forge a path toward financial independence and personal growth. For many, the journey into network marketing is not just about economic gain but also about personal development, community building, and realizing one's potential beyond the constraints of a 9-to-5 job.

But before we delve deeper into the intricacies of this dynamic field, let's set the stage with some captivating anecdotes that highlight the essence of network marketing. Imagine, if you will, a vibrant mosaic of individuals from all walks of life, which is united by a shared vision of success. These individuals come from diverse backgrounds, each with their own unique strengths, passions, and aspirations. Some may be seasoned entrepreneurs, while others may be venturing into the business world for the first time.

Despite their differences, they are all drawn to network marketing for its transformative power. They recognize the potential to not only achieve financial prosperity but also to cultivate meaningful relationships, contribute to their communities, and leave a lasting impact on the world. These individuals are not merely chasing a paycheck; they are embarking on a journey of empowerment, self-discovery, and limitless possibilities.

As we embark on this exhilarating journey together, let us embrace the spirit of network marketing, cherishing the personal connections we forge along the way. Let us celebrate the successes, both big and small, and learn from the inevitable setbacks that may arise. It is through these experiences that we grow, evolve, and ultimately achieve the success we seek.

So, dear reader, prepare yourself for an adventure like no other. Welcome to the world of network marketing, where dreams take flight and personal fulfillment awaits. Let us embark on this journey together, unlocking the true potential that lies within each of us.

The Business Model Explained

Hello there, let's explore the dynamic realm of network marketing! It's an exceptional business model where you can excel without requiring a high school diploma. How incredible is that? You don't need a formal degree to thrive in network marketing—it's all about your determination, diligence, and enthusiasm for the products.

Moreover, in network marketing, anyone has the potential to become a multi-millionaire. It genuinely doesn't matter where you originate or what your upbringing entails. If you're committed to putting in the effort and cultivating strong relationships, the possibilities are limitless. It's about crafting your personal success narrative, irrespective of your ethnicity, gender, or identity. How empowering is that?

Here's the scoop: in network marketing, you're not just promoting products. You're establishing a fantastic team of like-minded individuals who share your enthusiasm for the products. It revolves around recruiting and guiding new members while fostering an energizing environment of progress and achievement. The larger and more dynamic your network, the greater the potential for passive income and advancement.

This is where multi-level marketing (MLM) enters the scene. It revolves around manifold compensation levels that recognize both sales and the construction of a thriving and efficient downline. Essentially, the more you expand your team and empower them to succeed, the greater your own achievements. It's a remarkable cycle of encouragement and expansion that can lead to remarkably gratifying outcomes.

Well, network marketing is all about evening the playing field and granting everyone the opportunity to script their success tale. It's not about your origins or appearance—it's about your dedication, your fervor, and your drive to materialize your aspirations. That's what makes it incredibly remarkable. If you're prepared to immerse yourself in this realm of possibilities, then prepare yourself for an exhilarating journey!

As newcomers navigate the waters of network marketing, it is vital to understand these strategies and the symbiotic relationship between selling, recruiting, and team empowerment, which ensures a thriving business.

Charting the Course to Success

The journey toward network marketing success is akin to captaining a ship; it requires vision, leadership, and a relentless drive to sail through uncharted waters. To stay the course, one must harbor an unyielding mindset and determination, qualities that serve as your compass towards achieving your personal and financial goals. The first step in this voyage is to immerse oneself in comprehensive training and mentorship programs offered by the network marketing company or successful mentors in the field. These resources are indispensable, as they provide the know-how and strategies necessary to effectively market products, build a robust network, and gracefully tackle obstacles.

Emphasizing personal development is equally crucial; network marketing is more than a business - it's a journey of self-discovery and self-improvement. As you expand your enterprise, you'll cultivate skills in leadership, time management, and resilience. The support of your upline and the community will be a guiding star, helping you forge ahead with confidence and purpose. As you learn and grow, you will progressively set and achieve higher goals, ensuring you're not only building a business but also shaping a legacy.

Understanding Payment Plans in Network Marketing

Network marketing offers a variety of compensation plans, each with its unique structure and method of reward. Understanding these plans is crucial for newcomers as it dictates how they will earn and grow within the company. Common plans include the uni-level plan, which allows you to recruit one line of distributors and pays out on a set number of levels; the binary plan, where you build two legs and your earnings are based on the weaker leg's performance; and the matrix plan, which limits the number of distributors you can recruit at each level, creating a structured downline.

Of special interest is the breakaway plan, particularly noteworthy for those just starting. This plan allows you to build a team of distributors beneath you and earn commissions based on the group's total sales volume. Once a member of your team meets certain criteria, they 'break away' to form their own group, and you may receive a percentage of their group's sales. This plan encourages not just sales but also the development of strong team members who can eventually lead their own groups. Beginners should look for a plan that matches their strengths and goals. A plan like the breakaway can be especially motivating, as it rewards you for both personal sales and the success of your team, providing an incentive to mentor and guide your downline effectively.

Potential for Growth and Rewards

The allure of network marketing lies in its potent promise of growth and financial rewards. The defining feature of this business model is the opportunity to earn residual income, a payment that continues to accrue long after the initial sale. This is the income that can liberate one from living paycheck to paycheck, creating a financial buffer that can resist economic downturns and personal emergencies, ultimately leading to financial freedom. Successful network marketers often recount their transformational stories, speaking of the life-altering impact of building a business that not only generates steady income but also affords them the luxury of time—to spend with family, travel, or pursue other passions.

Imagine the empowering feeling of creating your success story, where your earnings reflect your efforts and your business grows even while you sleep. The key to unlocking these rewards lies in persistence, a keen understanding of the market, and a commitment to nurturing your downline—the network of distributors you help to flourish. By doing so, you can ascend to levels of achievement where financial constraints become a thing of the past and a world of opportunities opens up right before your eyes.

Chapter 1:
Setting Achievable Goals

"Begin with the end in mind." - Stephen Covey.

This quote from Stephen Covey emphasizes the importance of setting clear and specific goals. Covey believed that in order to achieve success, it is essential to have a clear vision of what you want to accomplish. By starting with the end in mind, you can align your actions and decisions with your ultimate objectives, leading to greater focus and effectiveness. Covey's quote serves as a reminder that goal setting is not just about creating a list of aspirations but rather about envisioning the desired outcome and working backward to determine the necessary steps to get there. It encourages individuals to consider their long-term objectives and then use those as a guide for their daily actions and choices. In essence, "Begin with the end in mind" urges individuals to be proactive and intentional in their goal setting, ensuring that their efforts are directed towards meaningful and purposeful outcomes.

In network marketing, setting realistic goals is the foundation for making things happen. When it comes to goals, think SMART: *specific, measurable, achievable, relevant, and time-bound.* This means having clear objectives, tracking progress, and ensuring that they are attainable within a set timeframe. Personal growth and self-improvement are key players in the goal-setting game. You've got to develop the skills and mindset to go after those objectives with everything you've got. And let's not forget about the power of mentorship and training programs. They're like your secret weapons, giving you the knowledge and strategies you need to chase your dreams. Overcoming personal barriers and building a tough mindset are non-negotiable. It's about powering through challenges and setbacks like "a boss on the road to success."

Defining Realistic Goals in Network Marketing

In the early '90s, I embarked on my first network marketing journey with Melaleuca, which was introduced to me by my fiance's uncle. He introduced me to the products and the compensation plan, igniting in me dreams of swift financial gains. I invested in the products and, for a while, rode the wave of initial enthusiasm. However, my motivation began to wane, and eventually, I realized why: *I had not established strong, realistic goals for my business.* The allure of quick wealth fascinated me; I envisioned purchasing everything I desired. Yet, when faced with the work essential to realize these dreams — allocating time daily, reaching out to potential clients within my circle, dialing number after number — the excitement drained away.

My inability to pursue my goals wasn't arbitrary. It stemmed from a childhood entrenched in socioeconomic hardship, where the concept of 'money' was erratic and laden with negative associations. In a household that saw income dissipate on vices, where the cycle of hand-to-mouth existence was the norm, discussions about earning or managing finances were alien concepts. I grew up with erratic sleeping schedules and no preparations for the next day's work because no one held a job. Consequently, a solid work ethic and financial acumen remained elusive to me.

Throughout my upbringing, and perhaps like some of your prospects, money epitomized both euphoria and crisis — fluctuating between joyous splurges and the stark reality of insufficiency. This duality fostered a distrust in money's reliability and its ability to secure stability. Hence, when presented with a network marketing opportunity primarily selling the 'get rich quick' narrative, it clashed with my ingrained perspectives and sabotaging narratives. I wasn't inspired to act because money, in my experience, was synonymous with transient happiness followed by disruption.

What is helping me grow in these early stages is figuring out my relationship with money and making adjustments. Whether you are a novice or an experienced network marketer who has achieved marginal success, it may be due to an unhealthy relationship with money or negative messages attached to money. As we identify our relationship with money, healing from hurt may need to happen, especially if some of the hurt experienced occurred because our parent(s) misused money or abused it to our detriment.

For those of us who hail from impoverished and marginalized backgrounds, it's not the lure of financial gain that captures our attention—it's the potential to break the cycle of inequity. What we yearn for is not just financial literacy but a transformation in our relationship with money. We need a re-education that distinguishes the mere possession of money from the obsessive pursuit of it, as it's the latter that cultivates harm. In my case, foundational goals like mastering time management, establishing clear objectives, nurturing a robust work ethic, and unlearning detrimental financial behaviors were crucial stepping stones that should've paved my path in network marketing.

Steps to Setting And Working Towards Your Goals

If my upline had been aware of the complexities in my past affiliations with people, finances, and vocations, they might have tailored a more fitting training program for my needs. Whether you're an experienced upline or a beginner, it's crucial to invest time in understanding your colleagues beyond the surface. Engage in genuine conversations. By temporarily setting aside the business agenda, you can glean insights into the personal trials and unspoken aspirations that often hinder newcomers like me, preventing us from fully embracing potentially transformative partnerships.

Many people who are entering the business, like me, have not experienced friendship or mentoring. Instead, we have been taught to be distrustful of people and conceal to protect ourselves from harm.

Many of us have experienced situations where people exploited our weaknesses. Due to these past experiences of others using our mistakes to shame or ridicule us, we tend to perceive suggestions for improvement as unhelpful criticism. When offering remarks aimed to help us improve, simply let us talk about the challenge or problem, then say, "I did this, and it worked for me when I was in a similar situation. Try it! It may just work for you, too." Always emphasize sharing your story. Sharing stories is the best teacher.

When encountering someone from a disadvantaged background whose historical connections with people and money have been fraught with challenges, take the time to truly connect. If you perceive a latent potential in them, endeavor to uncover it. The individual before you may possess a latent spark; if so, your task is to nurture it into a blaze. Encourage them to articulate their objectives and revisit these written goals regularly. In doing so, you're not merely instructing them to dream but to engage with their ambitions actively. Listen intently to their reasoning behind these ambitions. Within their narratives, you will find the keys to their requisite training. Direct them toward the appropriate resources and literature that will catalyze their development. Remember, it's often not monetary gain but rather the unacknowledged dreams that fuel their perseverance. By lending an ear to these dreams, you illuminate the path for both of you.

Chapter 2:
Learning from Your Upline

I once came across a quote by Robert Kiyosaki that left a lasting impression. He stated, *"The wealthiest individuals in the world build and cultivate networks, unlike others who seek employment."* This quote made me contemplate the significance of a strong upline in the field of network marketing. Having a mentor who has overcome challenges and is willing to provide guidance through the journey can be crucial. It's akin to having a supportive mentor who can assist you in traversing the complexities of the industry. It's undeniable that a dependable upline holds considerable importance in this arena.

My venture into Amway marked another chapter in

my network marketing journey. It highlighted to me that there's a significant, yet often overlooked, segment of the MLM market that doesn't conform to traditional expectations. They may possess unique dialects that don't resonate typically or harbor attitudes seemingly unaligned with success and wealth. As one who emerged from such a demographic, I assert that our patriotic spirit and the pursuit of the American dream are no less fervent; however, the mindset of poverty and the gap in accessible mentorship is palpable. There was a time when community role models were just a doorstep away, but with the migration of professionals to more affluent areas, capable mentors became scarce.

Entering Amway, my skepticism towards authority figures cast a shadow on the mentor-upline dynamic. Previous negative experiences had taught me to eschew their guidance, undermining the potential insights, wisdom, and expertise they offered. In my interactions, I offered a facade of openness and trust, whereas my behavior spoke volumes of my inner resistance and avoidance.

The Role of the Upline in Network Marketing

Yet, amidst this internal turmoil, I encountered an extraordinary mentor couple while I was developing my parenting and anger management practice. They were the epitome of knowledge, benevolence, and professionalism. Our meeting around 2015 was serendipitous, but due to unresolved issues from my past, their tutelage slipped through my fingers. My inability to embrace their guidance led to a gradual distancing, yet it wasn't without lessons learned. What resonated with me was not just the potential of network marketing as a business model but also the realization of the importance of personal growth, trust-building, and overcoming past barriers to truly benefit from mentorship.

In the landscape of network marketing, the upline is the lighthouse within the tumultuous seas of enterprise. Their role extends far beyond mere recruitment or salesmanship; they stand as the custodians of aspiration, the architects of achievable goals, and the guiding force ushering in a cascade of successes for those who are willing to learn and grow.

For those of us who tread through the maze of network marketing, the upline is akin to the mentor we might never have had in our neighborhoods, devoid of professional inspiration. They fill a void left by society's shifting tides, providing a beacon to those thirsting for direction and exemplifying the values and work ethic that can propel us toward the dreams we harbor—dreams fueled by equal parts hope and the quintessential American spirit.

But the mantle of an upline is not without its complexities. It demands not only business acumen but also an empathetic touch—the wisdom to navigate the unique tapestry of backgrounds everyone brings to the table. The upline's expertise must be paired with intuition to discern and adapt to the subconscious signals of those they mentor, often providing support in uncharted emotional territories.

My encounters with my uplines, especially the remarkable couple I met while crafting my journey, have further etched in my mind the significance of such a role. They exuded professionalism, warmth, and an earnest desire to uplift. Yet, it was not their fault that my unresolved past became a barrier to absorbing the full spectrum of their mentorship. Looking back, it's clear that the upline's role is multifaceted but woven with a common thread — the intention to build not just business prowess but to sculpt resilient characters.

The ideal upline recognizes that network marketing is more than a platform for financial gain; it's an opportunity for comprehensive personal development, for charting a course through lives that have seen more valleys than peaks. A great upline does more than impart strategies for success; it helps resurrect the esteem that may have been worn down by life's relentless undulations, transforming distrust and disenchantment into confidence and strategic optimism.

As succeeding in network marketing calls not only for expertise but for genuine human compassion, the upline must deftly weave together the strands of professionalism and personal connection, creating a tapestry that exemplifies the best of what network marketing can achieve. It's about nurturing a sense of self-worth that enables individuals to transcend former limitations and redefine their narratives with their newfound acumen.

How to Analyze and Learn from Their Strategies

Ultimately, the upline's role in our grand venture is unfolding as a beacon of leadership, where they're currently leading by example, actively imparting knowledge, and crucially, instilling in us the firm belief that we can each achieve our entrepreneurial visions. It's a path we're traveling together, a collective journey that sees our successes weaving into the broader dream we're all striving for.

Right now, as I navigate through the intricacies of network marketing, I'm finding immense value in being both a diligent student and an introspective learner. This twofold approach is anchoring my process of growth, allowing me to draw meaningful conclusions from the shared victories and trials faced by my various uplines.

In dissecting their strategic approaches, I'm currently examining the structures they have in place—the ways they're managing their networks, stimulating sales, and addressing challenges. I'm not just fascinated by the mechanics of their operations; instead, I'm delving into the psychological drivers that underpin the success of their relationships. I am learning to emulate the profound connection-building that they model, to turn my contacts into lifelong business allies.

To fully integrate these valuable lessons, I am actively immersing myself in the experiences my uplines are offering. I am currently attending their events with focused intention, taking in every detail of how they present and interact. The stories they're sharing are what I'm keenly listening to as I strive to perceive how each narrative fits within the grander scheme of successful entrepreneurship. I'm beginning to mimic their craft in my storytelling, meticulously infusing my experiences with the same degree of resonance.

Engaging in dialogue with my uplines—whether in person, virtually during training, via group chats, or through text messaging—is forming a crucial component of my educational experience. I'm reaching out not simply for advice but to cultivate a deep understanding of their strategic motivations and rationales. Every strategy, every tidbit of advice, is serving as a live thread that's currently being integrated into the bigger patchwork of my profession. As I reflect on these dynamic exchanges, I'm adapting their hard-earned wisdom to my unique circumstances and pondering how their insights can inform my strategies. I am now coming to appreciate that the setbacks my uplines have faced are proving just as instructional as the wins they're celebrating. I'm learning to view these moments as openings for constructive development—recognizing each challenge as a chance for me to cultivate my resilience and hone my practices further.

Keeping records has become an essential element of the journey I'm on. By documenting my ongoing observations and inner musings, I'm compiling a tangible log of my progress—a customized playbook that's taking shape from the fusion of my mentors' experience and my reflective process.

Grasping the strategies of my upline is akin to getting into the rhythm of a novel dance. With each step I'm taking, I'm gradually incorporating their teachings into the core of my network marketing approach. It's a continuous phase of refinement, where every lesson learned is actively propelling me towards a symphonic climax of my business endeavors.

Chapter 3:
The Power of Humility

"The most important thing is to try and inspire people so that they can be great in whatever they want to do." I think that really speaks to the role of humility in success. Being humble allows you to learn from others — Kobe Bryant.

This quote speaks to the heart of humility. It says to me, "Stay grounded, and keep pushing yourself to be better." It's not about being boastful or thinking you're better than everyone else; it's about recognizing that there's always room to grow and improve. So yeah, I'd say humility is pretty darn important when it comes to achieving success.

If your journey mirrors mine, you too, have emerged

from the shadows of childhood trauma, a legacy etched by relationships with influential adults— perhaps a distant mother, an indifferent father, or other guardians. These early figures in our lives unintentionally transmitted a gnawing void, a sense of unwelcomeness, and a feeling of being unloved. Our small world was often shrouded in neglect, and our cries for the most basic of needs—food, warmth, and safety—were left unanswered, breeding a profound sense of anger.

This anger, for those of us sharing this path, manifested in different ways. Some of us lashed out, bristling with hostility towards those we saw as authority figures, while others, like myself, learned to coil this anger inward. This was a survival tactic to avoid provoking a hostile reaction from those who might grow weary or irritated by our pleas for attention.

We chose silence over outcries, hoping against hope that our quietened sobs would somehow beckon a comforting presence to our side. And, like me, you might have found that any show of vulnerability only summoned further rejection, isolation, or even anguish. To survive was to wear a chameleon's skin, adapt, and become what was necessary to avoid the sting of neglect.

Life was not about thriving but about finding a way through each day unscathed. Curiosity could be perilous; revealing bewilderment or acknowledging confusion was an invitation for rebuke or harm. So, we feigned comprehension, nodding along even as we floundered in silent bafflement. We feared vulnerability would lead to beratement or shaming.

Our past left us with an abiding lesson: vulnerability is a risky venture that could unfurl the sail of reprimand or shame, setting us adrift once more. Thus, we built formidable ramparts of perceived ability, independence, and self-sufficiency. Behind these walls, we cultivated an aura of capability and competence that belied our true needs. The ultimate act of defiance against our beginnings—refusing to concede that we might require assistance.

Finding Strength in Personal Belief Systems

Within the crucible of building an organization, by those who have my history, vulnerability is often cloaked in bold displays of false bravado and common displays of superficial competence. We focus our attention on our appearance and status. Yet, it is the enlightened upline who can see through us, and their habit of humility shows us that mistakes and momentary hiccups are normal and a natural part of the growth process. With humility as a bedrock of strength, we always come back wiser, stronger, and more prosperous. Envision an upline who doesn't merely lead from a lofty perch but strides beside you as an example of what they preach, recognizing that humility is not a weakness but the very essence of strength, providing reassurance and comfort through their belief system.

These mentors, sculpted from trials akin to our own, have honed a philosophy in which they perceive the business storm as more deftly steered with empathy and genuine connection. Rather than casting a long shadow, they act as a keystone for our advancement, inspiring their team to value humility and showing through action that listening, learning, and serving others represent the pinnacle of business insight.

For such a leader, humility is an intrinsic philosophy, prioritizing the quiet rhythm of teamwork over lone victory celebrations and understanding that in the chorus of collaboration, each voice, however gentle, is vital to harmony. Their missteps are shared not as a weakness but as a beacon of their dedication to perpetual betterment and respect for the collective journey.

They foster our bravery to acknowledge our flaws not with scorn but with a determination to improve. The upline knows well the immense strength required to stand bare, leaving behind the guise of perfection and instead showcasing a heart of tenacity and collective success. In the subtle power of humility, they shepherd us, proving that within the nurturing ground of transparency and teamwork, we plant the seeds of lasting success.

I stand at the threshold of accepting my vulnerability, coaxing myself toward the once unthinkable act of accepting help. Despite the familiar hushed tones of caution and remnants of past rejection, I gradually embrace a supportive inner monologue. This internal dialogue acts as both a reminder and a vow — that the fear that once halted my progress is now just a specter of the past.

With care, I am learning to relax my guarded defenses to offer peace to my lingering doubts. A new narrative is unfolding, where seeking the guidance of my upline marks not a setback but the beginning of a united effort to bolster my business.

Clutching at a facade of competence and enshrining silence as if it were a revered relic does little to nurture the growth I so deeply crave. Rather, it is by embracing vulnerability and seeking wisdom that I carve a path to genuine progress and the fulfillment of my ambitions. This transformation transcends a mere strategic pivot; it heralds an awakening to the reality that in unity, with a confluence of collective insights and shared endeavors, we stand immensely stronger than I could alone. The trajectory before us is unobstructed: relinquish the pretenses, reach out, and partake in a symbiotic journey to construct an enterprise underpinned by authentic rapport and collaborative reinforcement.

Humble Approaches to Learning and Growth

For the uplines mentoring someone who's walked in my shoes, here's a piece of advice: *Set clear expectations.* Encourage us to voice our needs, to be forthright, and to take the reins of our development. It's crucial not to indulge in any displays of powerlessness, self-defeating behavior, or neglect as these behaviors may be exhibited from time to time at the outset as trust in the uplines leadership builds.

Address such behaviors with intention and earnest concern, and challenge any notion of helplessness with candor. The truth we require should be unvarnished yet delivered without personal bias—straightforward yet with a tone that considers our past. Each correction should be accompanied by affirmation, a steady assurance of your investment in our successes.

When mistakes occur, as they inevitably will, our upline should make clear that the impetus is on us to navigate through them with their support. However, the knowledge that you stand ready with sagacious advice tempers the sting of errors, aiding the process of learning and correction. For individuals like myself, who grapple with the weight of shame or the trepidation of acknowledging faults, we're faced with a pivotal choice: to remain entrenched in our tribulations or to stretch out and rise. I am betting on the fact that YOU are of the latter as you are reading this book!

While the upline extends their hands, our vigor must catalyze our ascent; we clutch onto their guidance for equilibrium, not for elevation. It's on us to activate our resolve as we advance; our upline is merely a mentor, not the architect, of our business. They do not construct our enterprise nor execute its operations—that power lies solely in our grasp. As we work our way through difficulties, stand up from falls, and find solutions to our problems, we grow.

By following the readings suggested to us, listening to our upline's story, and following their example and advice, a path to success opens before us, paving the way to prosperity. Following in the footsteps of our upline takes us to success. Celebrating our wins establishes good habits and good accomplishments and builds a track record of achievements.

Chapter 4:
Spiritual and Moral Support

You know, I've come to realize the importance of spiritual and moral support in network marketing. Looking back at my first two tries, I can see now that the lack of a strong sense of purpose and personal values really held me back. Without those, I just couldn't focus my energy in the right direction. I'm starting to see that having a solid spiritual foundation and being surrounded by morally upright people is key to staying motivated, especially when things get tough. I mean, I met so many great folks in my company who fit the bill, but because I was too proud to admit I needed help, I missed out on their support. But this time around, I'm intentionally surrounding myself with positive and uplifting people, and let me tell you, it's making a world of difference. I've learned that having that kind of support system is crucial for success in network marketing. And you know what? I think I might be onto something here. It's not just about making money; it's about doing it in a way that aligns with my beliefs and makes me feel good about what I'm doing. So, maybe I'm not a big shot yet, but I can definitely see myself making some waves in the network marketing community with this emphasis on the importance of spiritual and moral support.

In the intricate tapestry of network marketing, spiritual and moral support are not merely adjuncts; they are the warp and weft that give it strength and texture. The pursuit of success in this domain is not a solitary endeavor but a collective symphony, wherein each individual's moral and spiritual fibers contribute to the organization's overall resilience and vibrancy.

Spiritual support, grounded in unwavering faith, provides an inner beacon that guides us through the mists of uncertainty and the tumult of competition. It offers a sense of purpose that transcends monetary gain, imbuing our daily actions with a profound significance. The shared spiritual ethos creates a bond that unites the organization, as members draw from a deep well of conviction and purpose that galvanizes their collective efforts.

Moral support, meanwhile, ensures that our climb is not devoid of conscience. In the dizzying heights of achievement, it is our moral compass that keeps us from straying from the paths of integrity and ethical conduct. It instills a culture where trust and respect form the bedrock of relationships, where success is not at the expense of another's downfall.

Together, spiritual and moral support create a fortifying framework. They encourage us to reach out during times of faltering faith and empower us to act with courage when faced with moral dilemmas. In an arena often marred by short-lived victories and transient alliances, these pillars stand as enduring testaments to what sets a truly cohesive and principled network marketing organization apart. It is in this nurturing environment that members flourish, not only as marketers but as individuals rooted in a deep sense of kinship and shared values.

Finding Strength in Personal Belief Systems

I must acknowledge with sincere transparency that this book would not exist without mentioning Jesus, who has been pivotal in my journey of self-improvement. The formative wounds of my childhood led to the creation of an artificial facade that masked underlying insecurities and a relentless self-critique. Rather than self-worth, my focus lay on external validation through status, looks, and competition, despite a deep-seated disdain for my features and a Nigerian heritage I now recognize as beautiful. Without a disciplined routine for study or practice, I settled for mediocrity, encapsulating both contradiction and complexity within my being.

Encountering Jesus did not magic away my troubles, but in seeking His forgiveness, I found solace and a profound sense of liberation. His teachings and a resonant inner voice urged me not to surrender to my failings, to see beyond the scars that impaired my judgment and fostered a victim mentality. My achievements today — this very book being one — are not the fruits of my labor alone. Jesus entered my heart at the tender age of thirteen, and while my transformation was not instantaneous, my faith in Him has taken root amid life's tumult.

Throughout the creation of this book, there have been struggles, yet His unwavering love and call to excellence have remained constant. Jesus has served as my compass through the adverse repercussions of my flawed decisions, guiding me toward a better self. It is in His love and the striving for greatness He imbues that I found the strength to overcome and the courage to pen these pages.

Regardless of your spiritual beliefs, grasping this truth is key to thriving in network marketing — it's a journey that requires faith. I would be remiss to suggest otherwise. Here, faith implies a heightened awareness, an unwavering confidence in our imminent success, and a profound belief that God desires our prosperity. It means envisioning our achievements before they materialize. Such faith connects us with the divine, fortifying our resolve in the face of adversity.

Faith isn't abstract; it's experiential, palpable, donned as armor for the soul. This faith is quantifiable and accessible, a wellspring within, ready to replenish us during times of need or uncertainty. It is our steadfast companion amid life's upheavals. When activated, faith infuses us with unyielding determination, perseverance, patience, concentration, and discipline.

This force awakens within us at our behest, a gift from God nestled in our spirit for such moments that demand its presence. As you embark on the voyage of network marketing, let faith be your steadfast guide.

Inclusive Discussion on Spirituality and Ethics

My observation has been that spirituality is deeply interwoven into the fabric of my uplines' successes in network marketing. As I absorbed their narratives, a shared thread emerged: a conviction that the Divine was instrumental in their journeys of expansion. Initially met with skepticism, they grew to believe that their prayers may have been answered through these newfound opportunities.

The thread of spirituality, woven into various labels such as serendipity, divine guidance, or synchronicity, seems to have been the guiding force drawing them toward their network marketing paths. Many recount standing at this pivotal junction amidst professional dissatisfaction, emotional turbulence, or a deficit of financial contentment, all seeking the sense of achievement missing from their current roles. Driven by this profound inner discontent that unsettled the very core of their being, they were compelled to leap into the business world, embarking on an exploration of possibilities.

What they unearthed was an unexpected discovery of deep and resonant connections with like-minded individuals. Along this journey, some found solidarity akin to brotherhood, while others cultivated bonds that mirrored sisterhood. But universally, they discovered a sense of family: a community forged on kinship and camaraderie, providing a sanctuary of shared values and mutual support within the dynamic landscape of network marketing.

Likewise, network marketing appealed to an inner sense of adventure. The travel stories, coaching others, sharing my story to inspire, vacationing in exotic places, traveling to romantic locals and sampling the cuisine, and enjoying the landscape all spoke to me and drew me in. I help improve others' lives while enjoying all the wonderful things this life has to offer at the same time. Each time the opportunity came, it was serendipitous. In moments when transformation beckoned with irresistible fervor, when a suffocating sense of restriction and the absence of joy loomed over me, the horizon of network marketing emerged as a beacon of change and freedom.

Despite the allure, grappling with my limitations, I hesitated at the threshold of liberation, unable to liberate myself from my circumstances. Each venture into this industry brought with it opportunities for profound personal growth—opportunities that, I must confess, I let slip through my fingers. An amalgam of low confidence, insecurities, and emotional upheaval, together with a distrust of authority, fear of judgment, and an inability to accept constructive criticism, conspired to weaken my steadfastness, leading me down a path lined with disenchantment and disillusionment.

I now recognize that the role of an upline extends into a moral sphere, where mentorship and emotional support are critical for helping newcomers navigate these same personal challenges. Accepting the inherent spiritual and emotional aspects of this journey compels network marketing to adopt an ethical framework—one that champions personal growth and bolsters individuals' ambitions, fostering a culture that esteems moral and spiritual progress alongside commercial success. The narratives spun by my uplines—tales not of ostentatious displays or elite origins but of authentic experiences from relatable, earnest lives—echo a profound truth.

Many hail from modest beginnings, sharing sage counsel grounded in reality rather than exaggerated claims of swift prosperity. My aspirations for immediate, effortless success clashed with the sobering reality of the industry: transformation through network marketing is a marathon, not a sprint. It requires a commitment to personal and spiritual self-development. I iterate. This is not a crash course. With a willingness to change, dedication, and systematic effort, it presents the potential for significant earnings. It's a pragmatic business, absent of fanciful boasts, offering credible projections for those willing to apply themselves diligently over time. Remember, don't compare your progress to others; temper your fervor with patience and set realistic goals for your progress. This is an industry where focus, kindness, hard work, working the numbers, serendipity, synchronicity, and divine guidance pay off!

Chapter 5: Recognition and Acceptance

You know, in the world of network marketing and prospecting, there's this saying that goes, "People don't care how much you know until they know how much you care." And it's so true! Recognition of someone's presence and acceptance of who they are is key in this game. I mean, think about it - when you make someone feel seen and heard, when you accept them for who they are, they're more likely to open up to you and to trust you. And that's huge in this business! Because, at the end of the day, it's all about building relationships, right? So yeah, recognizing the presence of others and accepting them for who they are is not just a nice thing to do; it's actually a game-changer in network marketing and prospecting. It's like the secret sauce that sets you apart from the rest. So next time you're out there trying to grow your network or find new prospects, remember the power of recognition and acceptance - it can take you a long way!

It's time we talk about a sensitive but critical issue that has permeated my experiences across network marketing environments— the nuanced recognition of presence. This isn't to cast aspersions on those I've worked with directly; rather, it's an acknowledgment of the subtle exclusions that can be all too common. In gatherings predominantly composed of white attendees, I've observed a troubling pattern in social interactions: an absence of eye contact and genuine acknowledgment when approaching or passing by others, in contrast to the warmth and receptiveness often extended amongst individuals of the same background.

This isn't an isolated feeling but a reflection of a broader dynamic where people of African descent can become acutely aware of differential treatment.

It's the chill of a handshake that lacks sincerity or the rigid politeness that fails to mask indifference. And for those belonging to historically marginalized communities, such gestures — or the lack thereof — resonate with a deeper disquiet, recalling memories of deliberate ostracization.

The path to inclusivity in network marketing, and indeed any community, begins with a conscious effort. When belonging to the majority, the onus is not only to be aware of implicit biases but also to actively counter them with intentional inclusiveness. This means making a concerted effort to greet, engage, and welcome those who may not share your appearance or background. It's about cultivating an atmosphere of harmony and open arms, sending a clear message that every person is valued and vital to the collective success.

Confronting these realities with empathy and awareness can carve a space for progress and unity. Only when we become adept at reading the room and radiating a genuine welcoming presence can we hope to move beyond the shadows of segregation's history and embrace the diverse tapestry that constitutes our shared humanity — and build stronger, more cohesive organizations.

Identifying Strengths and Areas for Improvement

To foster an atmosphere of inclusivity in network marketing, practitioners can adopt several practical steps. These strategies leverage existing strengths and address areas that require improvement, ensuring that every person feels welcomed and valued.

Strengths to Build On:

1. **Diversity Awareness Training:** Initiate programs that educate members on the significance of inclusivity and the impact of subtle biases. Such training taps into the existing willingness of individuals to learn and grow and channels it toward fostering a more welcoming environment.

2. **Diverse Representation:** Continue to highlight and promote the success of individuals from a variety of backgrounds. Representation is a powerful tool that not only inspires but also normalizes diversity within the organization.

Areas for Improvement:

1. **Active Engagement:** Create structured opportunities for interaction, like mentorship programs that pair newcomers with experienced members from different backgrounds. This breaks down invisible barriers and encourages genuine connections.

2. **Feedback Mechanisms:** Establish channels for transparent communication where members can voice concerns and experiences regarding inclusivity. Listening and acting upon feedback demonstrates a commitment to continuous improvement.

Actionable Steps:

1. Implement a 'buddy system' to pair new members with friendly faces who can guide them through their first events.

2. Organize social mixers that celebrate cultural diversity and encourage open dialogues.

3. Recognize and reward acts that exemplify inclusivity, reinforcing positive behaviors.

4. Conduct regular reviews of meeting dynamics and make adjustments to ensure equitable engagement.

By committing to these practical steps, network marketing organizations can move towards a genuinely inclusive culture that recognizes and embraces the unique contributions of all its members.

The Importance of Self-awareness in Business Success

The importance of self-awareness in the context of network marketing cannot be overstated — the ripple effect it has on business success is both profound and multifaceted. Self-awareness serves as the cornerstone for building strong relationships and fostering effective leadership within the business. This introspective ability enables individuals to attune to their inner strengths and weaknesses, shaping a more mindful approach to interactions and business strategies.

Self-aware leaders can navigate the intricacies of their teams' dynamics, leveraging their insights to maximize each member's potential. This holistic understanding promotes emotional intelligence, allowing for more meaningful engagements and creating a resilient, empathic culture. When leaders embody self-awareness, they become the beacon of authenticity, inspiring trust and nurturing loyalty in their ranks.

Moreover, the presence of self-awareness ensures that emotional regulation becomes a practiced skill, vital in the ever-fluctuating climate of network marketing, where one's reaction can significantly sway team morale and output. It's about leading not only with intellect but with heart—engaging with a sincerity that resonates and motivates.

Self-awareness also fosters ethical consciousness. It directs individuals to reflect on the wider impact of their actions, prioritizing equitable interactions and comprehensive support systems that bolster every team member, reflecting an inclusive ethos.

By incorporating self-awareness into training modules and development, network marketing organizations can build leaders who are not only cognizant of potential blind spots but are also actively committed to countering implicit biases. Such initiatives empower organizations to acknowledge and celebrate diversity as a valued treasure.

Ultimately, self-awareness in network marketing is about aligning business practices with moral clarity and integrity. It's an ongoing dedication to examining both personal and professional dimensions, ensuring that the business grows not only in wealth but also in-depth and character. Through self-awareness, network marketing finds its true north—where success is measured not in monetary gains alone but in the flourishing of individuals and communities alike.

Chapter 6:
Visualization Techniques

There are numerous renowned quotes emphasizing the influence of visualization. One that resonates with me is by Albert Einstein, who famously remarked:

"Imagination is key. It provides a preview of forthcoming realities."

Essentially, this highlights how our mental images can materialize into our actual experiences. David Imonitie says about visualization, well, he's all about it. He's a big believer in the idea that:

"If you can see it in your mind, you can hold it in your hand."

He's all about using visualization techniques to

manifest your dreams and goals. So, if you ask me, it's pretty clear that visualization is a big deal!

Visualization is a game-changer in my pursuit. It's all about creating clear mental images of my goals and mapping out the steps to get there. When I visualize success, I boost my focus, motivation, and performance. In network marketing, I believe this technique is gold. I picture myself confidently connecting with potential clients, presenting products like a pro, and building strong relationships within my network. This mental rehearsal keeps me fired up and in the zone, which is key for making it big in network marketing. When I meet someone and begin speaking, it comes out effortlessly because I have been practicing it so much in my mind virtually. I don't underestimate the power of visualizing my network's growth and hitting those big milestones, as I believe that continuing this practice will eventually produce results. It's like giving myself a roadmap to success. By weaving visualization into my daily routine, I'm tapping into my imagination to drive myself toward those goals.

Using Visualization as a Tool for Achieving Success

Here's a visualization technique I call mapping. It all starts with picturing a future scene where I'm living out what I desire. I begin by imagining my morning routine, doing all the familiar things I'd normally do. As the day unfolds in my mind, I focus on the fact that I'm about to experience my deepest desires. It's like planning out the entire day in detail, step by step. The more detailed, the better. And as I keep visualizing, something amazing happens – it turns into a lucid dream. I get so immersed in this dream that it feels like real life. Eventually, I drift off to sleep, and the dream seamlessly continues from where the lucid dreaming left off. That's what mapping is all about – creating a super-detailed visualization that turns into a lucid dream and then transitions into a sleeping dream.

Practical Exercises for Goal Achievement

To support you in developing practical visualization skills to use in network marketing, based on the concept of "mapping" described above, here are six practice exercises tailored to help you.

1. "Desired Outcome Visualization":

Visualize a specific desired outcome in detail, focusing on the sensory aspects of the experience. Immerse yourself in the scene and mentally rehearse the steps leading to the achievement of your goal.

Visualization

Picture this: You're standing in a vibrant, bustling room filled with eager faces and an electric buzz of excitement. The air is charged with anticipation as you prepare to present your network marketing venture. Take a moment to visualize the scene vividly - notice the warm glow of the room's lighting, the hum of conversations, and the palpable energy surrounding you. As you step forward, a surge of confidence propels you, and your words flow effortlessly, captivating your audience. You can almost feel the genuine connections forming as you share your vision and the value of your products. Every detail is crystal clear – the smiles of approval, the nods of understanding, and the sense of empowerment filling the room. This visualization exercise isn't just about imagining success; it's about immersing yourself in the experience, feeling the excitement, and mentally rehearsing each step towards achieving your goal.

2. "Routine Visualization":

Visualize your daily routine, incorporating elements related to your network marketing activities. This exercise will help you mentally prepare for the tasks and interactions involved in your business.

Visualization

Imagine waking up to the soft glow of the morning sun filtering through your window, filling the room with warmth and promise. As you start your day, visualize the familiar routine of energizing activities – a refreshing morning walk, a nourishing breakfast, and a moment of quiet reflection to set your intentions for the day ahead. Now, picture the seamless integration of network marketing into your daily rhythm. Envision engaging in purposeful conversations with potential clients, sharing the value of your products with genuine enthusiasm, and cultivating meaningful connections within your network. See yourself navigating through tasks with ease, feeling confident and empowered in every interaction. This visualization exercise isn't just about envisioning your routine; it's about mentally preparing for the tasks and interactions involved in your business, infusing each moment with purpose and clarity. The mind does not distinguish between what we imagine we do and what we actually do, especially when we commit to whatever it is that we imagine. Imagined experience is stored in the same place as actual experience. What we routinely imagine becomes the equivalent of actual experience.

3. "Goal Progression Visualization":

Visualize the progression towards your goal, step by step. You should vividly imagine each milestone and the actions required to reach them, creating a mental roadmap toward success.

Visualization

You're imagining embarking on a journey towards your network marketing goals. You're visualizing each milestone as a stepping stone leading you closer to your vision. Is your milestone 10 front-line leaders or building deep with a customer base? Is an objective along the way to balance your legs between customers and distributors? Perhaps your goal is the next level up? You're talking to your upline and picking one of them to emulate. You're asking her to work with you to develop realistic objectives and goals. You're seeing yourself celebrating the small victories you mark off as milestone achievements – the successful client interactions, engaging small group presentations, the growth of your network, and the incremental progress towards your ultimate objective. You're envisioning the actions required to reach each milestone, making them all the more realistic because you've based them upon experiences that have been shared with you from your upline. You're creating a mental roadmap towards success. You're picturing the dedication, the resilience, and the strategic decisions that propel you forward. As you vividly imagine each step, you feel the sense of fulfillment and empowerment that comes with making progress. This visualization exercise isn't just about envisioning your goals; it's about immersing yourself in the journey, embracing each milestone, and mentally preparing for the actions that will lead you to success. You're seeing it happening to you before you do it for you.

4. "Lucid Dream Visualization":

The lucid dream is a visualization technique. Practice transitioning from a conscious visualization into a lucid dream state, where you can continue to focus on your network marketing aspirations. This technique I use is called *Bridging*. It's a fun way to prompt your subconscious to dream about conscious visualization. Consciously creating imagined scenarios is a powerful technique for network marketing success. By repeatedly practicing practical and realistic visualization scenarios, we can prompt our unconscious mind to pick up where our conscious visualization left off when natural dreaming begins. This process essentially tricks the subconscious into continuing the conscious dreaming sequence.

Visualization

As we immerse ourselves in the vivid details of our lucid dream, visualizing our network marketing goals and aspirations ideally when we lay down to sleep before we drift off to sleep or before we rise from the bed just as we wake from sleep in this drowsy state, we may be able to trigger a short dream sequence based upon our lucid dreaming. This is what I call bridging. We're laying the groundwork for our unconscious mind to seamlessly carry on this dream. This technique allows us to prompt our unconscious so that we give ourselves a guided dream specific to our lucid dream. We are reinforcing our goals and creating a seamless bridge between conscious and unconscious visualization. It's about engaging in a practice that enriches our mindset, aligns our actions with our aspirations, and sets the stage for practical and achievable success in network marketing. Rather than going out and making mistakes in our presentations to others, I propose that we spend more time visualizing and doing it the right way to make it second nature so that we simply execute fluidly publicly what we have been visualizing routinely privately.

The following are steps to creating and practicing lucid dreaming:

Step One:

Consciously create an imagined scenario. Use the mapping technique described earlier. Map out a scenario rich in detail.

Step Two:

Erase. Repeat. Re-create the same scene. Erase. Re-create it again. By repeatedly practicing visualization scenarios, we create an experience. We can prompt our unconscious mind to pick up where our conscious visualization left off as natural dreaming begins.

Step Three:

As you visualize, count backward from 99 to 0. If you drift to sleep before the count, that's okay. This takes practice. Eventually, you will introduce enough prompts into the subconscious to affect what you dream about. Your dream will find you in situations and scenarios where you are overcoming something. Winning at something and achieving something. In other words, your dreams will begin to become encouraging. That is what I am experiencing.

Step Four:

During the day, contact an upline and ask them to tell you their story. Listen to as many stories of success as possible. With each story you hear, visualize yourself in their shoes, experiencing the things they are experiencing and working through the problems. In this way, you convince your mind that what happened to them on their journey can also happen to you. In other words, the more you can relate to your upline journey, the greater your belief and conviction that it can happen for you.

I am using that visualization regime daily, and I hope that by engaging in this practice, I experience transformation and that my faith, esteem, focus, mindset, and actions are enriched and aligned with my aspirations, setting the stage for practical and achievable success in network marketing. My thinking is that the beginning of my breakout starts with the conscious decision to immerse myself in vivid mental scenarios that reflect my network marketing goals. As I engage in this practice, I believe I am cultivating a mindset that is attuned to success, fostering a sense of clarity, purpose, and determination. This deliberate focus on my aspirations serves as a compass, guiding my actions and decisions toward the realization of my goals.

It's about aligning my daily efforts with the larger vision I hold for my network marketing endeavors, ensuring that every action contributes to the broader tapestry of success I aim to achieve. I foresee that this practice is creating a fertile ground for practical and achievable success, instilling in me the resilience, resourcefulness, and strategic acumen needed to navigate the dynamic landscape of network marketing. Thus far, it has been an enriching and empowering journey that is not only shaping my professional endeavors but also nurturing my personal growth and fulfillment. In Chapter 7, I will share thoughts and insights I gained from reading David Imonitie's book *Conceive, Believe, Achieve: Create A Burning Desire Master the Skills To Win Work in Faith.*

Chapter 7:
David Imonitie: Conceive, Believe, Achieve

"...I learned what I now teach–that [we] must begin with the end in mind. I had a clear picture of what the end result already looked like." ~ David Imonitie

In the YouTube video channel, Jason C. Hannah posted the video *Desire + Skill x Faith = Success*. So, let's summarize this video. David Imonitie talks about what it takes to be successful in anything we do.

First off, we have to have that burning desire deep down inside. Like, we really have to want it, you know? And then, of course, we have to have the skills to back it up. It's like, we can want something all day long, but if we don't have the skills to make it happen, then we're just spinning our wheels. And hey, let's not forget about faith. We have to believe in ourselves and in what we're doing. It's like having that unwavering confidence that we're going to make it happen no matter what. Oh, and surrounding ourselves with people who have already achieved what we're after? That's a game-changer. We can show you the ropes and give you the inside scoop on how to get where you want to go. Also, he says, positive affirmations are no joke. I'm talking about telling ourselves every day that we're going to crush it, no matter what. Last but not least, persistence [perserverance] is key. We have to keep pushing forward, even when things get tough. That's the lowdown on how to make success happen in any field.

Here are a few key points from each chapter in his book *Conceive, Believe, Achieve: Create A Burning Desire Master The Skills To Win WORK IN FAITH:*

Chapter One: His Story

Like many of us, David started out in networking marketing, full of aspiration for a life of affluence and influence. Just like many of us, he hit a few walls and ran out of steam. In his own words: Things weren't working out like I thought they would, and I wasn't getting what I wanted. In my first two attempts at the business, I too, wanted quick results. Perhaps it was the simplicity conveyed in the presentations or the fact that the path to money seemed different, less structured, and less routine than a job. I had a picture in my head that all I had to do was present this product, and people would fall all over themselves to get it. Reality set in after my first several calls and criticisms from family members that this would not be easy. I did not understand that hard work, dedication, persistence, and perseverance are essential to success in network marketing. So, I dropped off slowly.

This point is made on page 5 of this book, David says:

"What you will read here is simple… But it isn't easy, and it isn't for those who aren't willing to do whatever it takes to make it happen."

Chapter Two: The Network Marketing Industry

This quote pretty much sums up chapter 2. David says, "I love the concept of really being able to help people get what they want out of life. I love the concept of being able to show people that it doesn't matter what your background is, it doesn't matter where you are from, it doesn't matter your race, your creed—anything like that." This business fits this Darwinian phrase aptly. It boils down to the survival of the fittest. The fittest arent the fiercest, strongest, the most educated, nor those from the best backgrounds. In my opinion, it is those who can make it, as David Imonitie says: "…until that survival breakthrough" happens. This is the emotional, mental, and spiritual breakthrough to the understanding that this business is all about "…helping other people understand that there's a process that they are going to have to go through--that it is going to allow them to get to where it is that they want to be." This excite about the manifestation of the person we conceptualize we will become increases daily as we meditate on it, as well as our excitement to help others become the person they conceptualize and meditate on daily. All this is reinforced by those around us who, from humble to average beginnings, having gone through the process, became the persons they conceptualized years before. Though not explicitly stated, David alludes to this essential quality—perseverance, something we all possess.

Chapter Three: Picture the End Result

The central idea of this chapter is that "...we must begin with the end in mind." According to David, this focus allowed him to stay in "the game" through adversity. Unlike me in my initial attempts, when I lacked a clear picture or vision of the person I wanted to be, David stated: "...This allowed him to keep pressing forward, to stay in the game..." This singular focus made it possible for him to easily clarify his goals, screen out distractions, and attract the people he desired to emulate. David relates this story of after having given a presentation to "...a couple 100's people about the opportunities they could have..." his sponsors dropped him off at the lobby of a hotel. After they left, he exited the lobby, walked to his car, which was parked a ways away, and slept in it. He says he did this many times during his first few years in the business. Because he had a clear vision of the person he desired to become, he was able to do this.

This is the most important technology, tool, ingredient, and mechanism—the proper use of the imagination to create pictures in the mind that affect our choices, which themselves create our experiences that shape our reality. In short, the mind creates reality! I have found, though I didn't realize or understand it at the time, my use of imagination to routinely depict hurt, loss, tragedy, etc., while not realizing that as I though about those who hurt me, often stirring up those feelings, I was reinforcing a victim mentality through visualization and keeping my mind populated with sorrowful things. I didn't understand that by doing this, I kept my focused in the past on hurt on the things that I lost or were taken from me rather than on the things I desired and could acquire. Earl Knightingale says that our mind acts like a servomechanism. What we routinely contemplate sinks into our unconscious mind to them affect, effect, influence, and manipulate our conscious thought and decision-making.

Chapter Four: Have a Mentor or Coach

"Humility is not a personality trait. It's just recognising that you don't have something." ~ David Imonitie

The above quote is chock full of insight gained from experiences acquired over time from the pursuit of worthy goals. A worthy goal is the culmination of the pursuit of an endeavor that requires active, passionate, focused attention to attain it. With that in mind, let's delve into what Mr. Imonitie says. He says that having a mentor or coach is essential. Somebody that we can "...actually call on–somebody that [we] can actually watch–is invaluable." Our mentor or coach is someone who is where we are heading. They have carved out a path, body of knowledge, and accumulated experience they can impart to a mentee or aspirant. The coach or mentor imparts their expertise so that we do not have to solve the same problems they encountered or surmount the same barriers they came up against. We obtain knowledge, wisdom, and insight that enables us to accelerate our progress.

Now, this does not mean our journey lacks credibility. On the contrary, we will be in similar situations, but now, we can draw upon their experience to meet those challenges. We meet the challenge, we apply the information, and we gain our own wisdom. We still encounter the same situations they experienced; however, we now spend less time wrestling with the challenge. The essential quality required on our part is humility, for without it, we do not own our deficiencies, acknowledge them, nor request help with them. As Mr. Imonitie says: "That's the deal. [We] must understand how to be humble and take the time to find a mentor and learn."

Chapter Five: Live In a Vision Environment

Surround yourself with reminders of where you are going. This means filling our environment with tangible representations of our future life and self. Our subconscious mind is always at work, picking up on things in the periphery of our consciousness. Even conversations can influence your subconscious. This means we should be playing in the background only things that speak to the person we seek to become at all times.

Living in our future environment means creating it now. It's like borrowing from the future to populate the present. In this atmosphere, whatever our senses detect in our periphery is transmitted to our subconscious mind, generating thoughts about it. As Mr. Imonitie says, "I put things around me that I want to become my reality." He is led by his thoughts — the thoughts he wants to have and the thoughts he considers. Just as Napoleon Hill meant by cultivating a burning desire, fires often start from tiny sparks and, when continuously fed, grow and spread. Similarly, Mr. Imonitie envisions that the spark within him is fueled by the physical representations of the things he surrounds himself with. So, let's fill our surroundings with inspiration and keep feeding that spark within us. As Napoleon Hill says, "We become what we think about."

Chapter Six: The Power of Belief

Understanding how our mind works is necessary. As we know, the environment plays a big role in shaping our personality and character. In like manner, what we surround ourselves with affects our emotional state. That's why, as many of us undergoing change have realized, if we are to experience the progression of change, we must get out of the environment that has nurtured our current state of mind because, as we continue in it, our current habits and mindset stay in play. Here is what David says about this: That is going to be key to our success. We've got to experience the desire. We've got to experience what it feels like...before it happens because if we don't experience it, we'll never believe it."

Mr. Imonitie calls this process CONCEIVING of our desire. This is the process of immersing our body and senses into an environment, be it an uplines house who lives in the kind of house we desire, visiting the car dealership and sitting behind the wheel of the car we desire, or finding a picture of the place we desire to visit and putting a cut-out of our body in the picture (easily done using photo editor app). We look at the picture until we can visualize it. We hold that image in our minds and then meditate on it routinely. These kinds of immersive experiences produce in us the corresponding feelings and emotions similar to what we would experience if we were there if we truly immerse our self in the visualization. Otherwise, we could imagine those feelings and then allow our self to experience them vicariously. "Once again, this conception part is just giving birth to an idea, giving birth to a vision—an environment. The whole key to that is our environment," says Mr Imonitie.

Chapter Seven: The Belief System

The belief system is simply this: live in the future while taking action in the present, then you will achieve the future you aspire to live in. "I always knew it was going to happen.", says Mr. Imonitie. I fill my present environment with pictures. I surround myself with people who show me its possible because they live it, and they tell me that I too, can have the same lifestyle. Not only that, but they provide me with the resources they accessed during their pursuit of their goals. With all these elements, I craft a self-portrait, a self-image that I focus on daily. David says, "How we see ourselves is how other people are going to see us."

Anything or anyone not supporting our newfound self-image or speaking positively to our self-portrait must be eliminated from our lives. We review our daily routine, looking for behaviors that do not support our self-portrait to eliminate them. We assess our thoughts for thinking patterns that do not support our self-image to eliminate them. Actively maintaining awareness of any mental pictures or thoughts that go against our belief system is a practice of literally apprehending those thoughts to destroy them. This may initially sound like an exhausting process, but consider how, in the past, we unconsciously allowed any willy-nilly thoughts triggering images of past hurt or pain to surface and run freely to the point that they affect our mood and attitude.

Recall how many times we found that we'd lost a whole hour just tripping over negativity. So, yes, at the outset, corralling those errant thoughts to restrain them from freely playing out in scenes of loss, hurt, or rejection will initially be taxing, but like any muscle we exercise, it will in time be effortless one day becoming instantaneous and instinctive. If we put in the work upfront and actively manage our new belief system, we will soon create a new kind of habitual thinking that keeps us focused, burning, and determined. I'll end here with this, "In the end, our imagination and vision are our choices; therefore, how we choose to move forward with our belief and action is also our choice," according to David Imonitie.

Chapter Eight: We Become What We Think About

Have you ever taken a moment to consider the power of our thoughts? The everyday stream of consciousness that flows through our minds, whether in the form of mental images or linked ideas, often reflects and reinforces our environment, education, culture, and daily habits. These thoughts are closely tied to our lifestyle, attitude, mood, and behavior. What we find interesting, entertaining, or captivating is a reflection of our habitual thought patterns. In essence, we are the culmination of our thoughts and mental images.

Our very identity is shaped by the continuous flow of our thoughts. It's a powerful realization that any change in our interests, habits, or commitments can lead to a transformation in our very being. As Mr. Imonitie aptly puts it, "I've become the person I am today based upon my thoughts. If I want to change something in my life, all I have to do is change my thoughts."

But where do our thoughts originate? They stem from our five senses. Does this mean that thoughts are floating around in the atmosphere, waiting to enter through our eyes, ears, taste buds, nose, and skin? Not quite. What we perceive through our senses enters as light, sound, substances, chemicals, and textures. These stimuli are then transmitted to our brain via the associated nerve pathways. Regardless of their initial form, they are ultimately converted into electrical impulses that travel to the central nervous system and onward to the brain. There, they are processed, interpreted, and associated with specific parts of our brain or past experiences.

For most people, their senses tend to dictate their experiences rather than the other way around. However, by consciously exposing our senses to experiences that align with the self-image and self-concept we aspire to cultivate, we can actively shape our own development. Through regular, targeted, and structured exposure to tailored information, we can bring to life the person we envision ourselves becoming. This deliberate approach allows us to nurture the growth of the individual we strive to be until it becomes the dominant personality within us.

Chapter Nine: How to Build a Network Marketing Organization

Alright, so now that we've got the self-concept, the environment, the mentoring and coaching, and the belief in place, let's talk about what comes next – the process. This is basically the steps we take to make our dreams a reality. Network marketing is the way we can achieve success and get the things we want in life. It's how we move towards our material, financial, health, and emotional goals. According to Mr. Imonitie, the first thing to understand is that this is a real business. It's not just network marketing or multi-level marketing; it's a legitimate way to make money and build our economic status. In this business, people are the capital. The more people we talk to, the more money we can make – simple as that.

Now, within the market of network marketing, there are different markets – the cold market, the warm market, and the hot market. The cold market is made up of people we don't know, like those we meet at the store or on public transport. The warm market is made up of people we know personally, like friends and family. And the hot market is basically anyone who has a connection to someone we know. Mr. Imonitie emphasizes that regardless of which market we're targeting, the key characteristics we should look for in people are humility, coachability, and teachability. He also suggests targeting people who are 25 and older, married, have children, own a home, and make an income of $40,000 – $80,000 per year. However, I believe there's a whole untapped market out there – people who may not fit these criteria but still have the potential to succeed in network marketing.

These individuals may have a humble spirit and be coachable and teachable, but for lack of education, low socioeconomic status, lack of employability, or personal or cultural reasons, they're often overlooked. I believe that network marketing can level the economic playing field for this untapped market by providing a way for anyone in this demographic to succeed, regardless of age or personal circumstances. As long as they can receive, believe, and act on the information provided and follow the steps with patience and perseverance, they can elevate their economic status. So let's keep it real, keep it open, keep it friendly, and keep working towards our goals to give this opportunity to anyone who is interested.

Chapter Ten: Prospecting

None of us knows initially who are the right people for this business except those who are in our warm market. We know substantially, based upon the demographic characteristics, who among them are most pre-qualified to get our calls. On the other hand, when it comes to our cold market, who can know at the outset who is qualified and who is not? As Mr. Imonitie says in his book, it is a numbers game.

If we talk to enough people, as he has said previously, we find that those who are most likely to be receptive to the business have 5 attributes in common, as laid out above. The failure he identifies is, "...most people fail in this business because they don't talk to enough people and they don't talk to enough of the right people." Let's talk about talking.

Talk is a form of communication that can take many different forms, including written, spoken, visual, and more. When it comes to reaching out to people in network marketing prospecting, it's important to consider the various ways in which we can "talk" to potential customers or recruits.

Written communication can take the form of emails, social media messages, or even blog posts. This can be an effective way to reach a wide audience and provide detailed information about products or opportunities. Spoken communication, on the other hand, might involve phone calls, in-person meetings, or even virtual presentations. This can be a more personal and engaging way to connect with individuals and build rapport. Visual communication, such as videos or infographics, can also be impactful in capturing attention and conveying information in a compelling way.

For someone starting out in network marketing, using social media as a platform for live presentations can be an effective way to "talk" to people about their product. By establishing themselves as an expert in their field through live presentations, they can showcase their knowledge and passion for the product while also engaging directly with their audience in real-time. This can help to build trust and credibility and ultimately attract potential customers or recruits who resonate with their message.

In conclusion, the way we "talk" to people in network marketing prospecting can vary greatly, and it's important to consider the most effective mode of communication depending on the audience. Whether it's through written, spoken, visual, or live presentations on social media, the key is to effectively convey the value of the product or opportunity while building authentic connections with others.

Key Insights From Conceive, Believe, and Achieve

So, this guy David started out in network marketing just like many of us, full of big dreams and high hopes. But then, reality hit, and things didn't go as planned. He wanted quick results, just like most of us did in the beginning. But he soon realized that it takes hard work, dedication, and persistence to succeed in network marketing. He dropped off for a while, but then he came back with a different mindset.

In his book, he talks about the concept of helping people achieve their goals, regardless of their background or where they come from. It's like survival of the fittest, but not in the traditional sense. It's about going through a process that allows you to become the person you want to be. It's all about having a clear vision of your end goal and staying focused on it.

David emphasizes the importance of having a mentor or coach to guide you through the process. Someone who has been where you want to go and can share their knowledge and experience with you. Humility is key here, as you need to recognize that you don't have all the answers and be open to learning from others.

Creating a vision environment is another crucial step. Surrounding yourself with reminders of where you want to be in the future helps to keep you focused and motivated. It's about living in your future environment now and immersing yourself in the experiences that will lead you to your desired outcome.

Belief plays a huge role in this journey. You have to experience the desire and truly believe in it before it can become a reality. It's all about shaping your thoughts and environment to align with your vision.

Your belief system is what drives you forward. Living in the future while taking action in the present is the key to achieving the future you aspire to live in.

It's about crafting a self-portrait and eliminating anything or anyone that doesn't support that self-image from your life.

We become what we think about, so it's important to be mindful of our thoughts and mental images. Our thoughts shape our personality, character, and ultimately, our reality. By consciously exposing ourselves to experiences that align with our desired self-image, we can actively shape our own development.

Now, when it comes to building a network marketing organization, it's essential to understand that this is a real business. People are the capital in this business, and the more people you talk to, the more money you can make. There are different markets to target, and it's important to look for humility, coachability, and teachability in potential recruits.

Prospecting is all about talking to enough of the right people. Whether it's through written, spoken, visual, or live presentations on social media, the key is to effectively convey the value of the product or opportunity while building authentic connections with others.

So, there you have it – David's journey and insights into network marketing. It's all about having a clear vision, surrounding yourself with the right people, and believing in yourself and your goals. And, of course, putting in the work to make it happen.

Key Lessons from Conceive, Believe, and Achieve

So, let's break it down. In Chapter One, David's story is pretty relatable. I mean, who hasn't hit a few walls and run out of steam at some point? It's like he said: things weren't working out as expected, and he wasn't getting what he wanted. I totally get that feeling of wanting quick results and then realizing that it's not as simple as presenting a product and having people fall all over themselves to get it. Reality can be a tough pill to swallow. But hey, he makes a good point about hard work, dedication, and perseverance being essential in network marketing.

It's not easy, but it's doable if you're willing to put in the effort.

Moving on to Chapter Two, the concept of helping people achieve their goals regardless of background or circumstances really resonates with me. It's like a survival of the fittest situation, but not in the traditional sense. It's about going through a process that allows you to become the person you want to be. I love the idea of manifesting the person we want to become and helping others do the same. It's all about perseverance and that emotional, mental, and spiritual breakthrough.

Chapter Three really hits home with the idea of starting with the end in mind. Having a clear vision of the person you want to become can really drive you to keep pushing forward. David's story about sleeping in his car after giving presentations really shows the level of commitment he had because of that clear vision. It's all about using your imagination to create the reality you want, and I can totally relate to not realizing the power of visualization in shaping our experiences.

In Chapter Four, David's quote about humility really stands out. It's not about having a certain personality trait; it's about recognizing when you need help. Having a mentor or coach is essential in any pursuit, and I can see how their guidance can help avoid common problems and accelerate progress. It's all about being humble enough to seek help and learn from those who have already walked the path.

Chapter Five talks about living in a vision environment, which is such an interesting concept. Surrounding yourself with reminders of where you're going and who you want to become can really influence your subconscious mind. It's like creating your future environment in the present, almost like borrowing from the future to shape your present. It's all about feeding that spark within you and filling your surroundings with inspiration.

Chapter Six delves into the power of belief, and it's so true that our mind and environment shape our emotional state. Immersing yourself in an environment that aligns with your desires can really create the corresponding feelings and emotions. It's all about experiencing what you want before it happens, and the process of conceiving your desires through immersive experiences is so powerful.

The belief system discussed in Chapter Seven is all about living in the future while taking action in the present. It's about creating a self-portrait and eliminating anything or anyone that doesn't support that self-image. It's like actively managing your new belief system and staying aware of any thoughts that go against it. It might sound exhausting at first, but it's all about creating new habitual thinking that keeps you focused and determined.

Chapter Eight really hones in on the idea that we become what we think about. Our thoughts are so powerful in shaping our personality, character, lifestyle, attitude, and behavior. It's amazing to think that any change in our thoughts can lead to a transformation in our very being. It's all about changing your thoughts to change your life.

In Chapter Nine, we get into the nitty-gritty of building a network marketing organization. It's all about understanding that this is a real business and that people are the capital. The market segmentation is interesting, but I also believe there's an untapped market out there for people who may not fit traditional criteria but still have the potential to succeed in network marketing.

Finally, Chapter Ten talks about prospecting and how talking to enough people is key. The mode of communication can vary greatly, from written to spoken to visual, but the key is to effectively convey the value of the product or opportunity while building authentic connections with others.

So there you have it – a breakdown of some key lessons from each chapter!

Chapter Eight:
People Are Capital

There is a Bible verse that says, "Money answereth all things."

Most of us understand that the more money we have, the more life we possess. This is something that even a child can grasp. The next thing we understand by experience alone is that money can come, and money can go. This can be illustrated simply by considering what happens to our allowance or paycheck. It came, then it went. Fundamentally, it became something we use, eat, wear, or occupy. So, we all understand that the more money we can come by, the more money we have in our possession to use. Considering the verse above in relation to the conversation we've just had, we certainly can do a lot with money rather than just spend it on ourselves, right? When we have enough money, we can help ourselves first, and then we can help others too, if we are so inclined. The more we have, the more people we can help! We can see that money can be used to help ourselves and help others, meaning, with enough money, we can make a difference in the world.

In the above, we have talked about the most common ways we receive money in exchange for labor. As an overview, money comes to us when we work for it. In exchange for our labor, someone will give us money. This is what we call employment. Now, can money be used to make money? Let's talk about that. We could take our money and start a business providing a product or service. This means that in exchange for our product or service, we receive money. We could invest the money from our business into another business, thereby owning multiple businesses that provide other kinds of products or services. This is money-making money. What about investing our money to own a percentage of another company, thereby becoming an indirect owner of a company? This is ownership based on purchasing shares of the company. Now we have stock in the company. We can own small or large portions of a company in this way. As the value of that stock grows, our money increases as the value of the stock grows. In this way, our money is making money without our labor or any exchange of a good or service. Regardless of the means by which we make money, there is one thing that these have in common.

None of us can make a dime without a human being involved. Remove the human being, no money. No product. No Service. No business(es). No corporation. No shares making increasing in value where our money is making money. Without human beings, there is no money, so it might as well be said: People are money and vice-versa. If we do not have a good relationship with people, we will not have money for long. Everything we have or own in life is because of people. Everything we have ever lost in life is by the same — people. Thus, it stands to reason that the better our relationships with people, the more money we will likely have access to or acquire. Now, there's one other element that has not been addressed. YOU! ME! We are people too. This may or may not come as a surprise, but if we do not have a good relationship with ourselves, we will not have a good relationship with other people or MONEY! By this, I mean if our self is damaged or broken (i.e., self-concept), we will be racked with many kinds of fears, anxieties, personality maladies, and self-sabotaging behaviors.

If you are reading this book, then you are at a level of personal development to understand that if we want more money, then we have to have to be able to establish good relationships with people and bring them value so that if in business, they will give us their money in exchange for the value our product or service brings them. This means we must be able to bring enough value to people so that they want to exchange the value they receive from us with the money in their possession. Our success hinges on this exchange with people. If we have a damaged self-concept and our insecurities, personality maladies, and self-sabotaging behaviors get in the way, causing us to mistreat people, no matter how much value our product or service brings them, they will be soured toward us and no longer transact with us. As for the product or service, they will go to someone else for it. The first thing we should do with money is use it for our own personal development. Why? Because "Money answereth all things." The first "thing" our money should help is us. If we are good, healthy, and whole in every sense of the word, then we will naturally build the kind of relationships that reflect the same. In this way, we will have the foundation upon which to build wealth and riches that are sustaining. More importantly, our self will not rest on people, worldly wealth, and riches but on the internal eternal abundance we uncover within from riches and wealth that abide forever.

Chapter Nine: Conclusion

In conclusion, "My Blueprint for Success: A Novice's Guide to Stepping onto the Path of Network Marketing Mastery" has taken you on a transformative journey through the fundamental principles of network marketing. From setting achievable goals to recognizing the importance of spiritual and moral support, each chapter has contributed to a holistic understanding of the industry.

The initial chapters laid the groundwork by introducing you to the core concepts of network marketing and guiding you through the process of setting goals that are not only ambitious but also attainable. Learning from your upline became a cornerstone, emphasizing the significance of mentorship, humility, and the power of genuine connections.

Chapter by chapter, you delved into the profound impact of humility and the role it plays in fostering meaningful relationships within the network marketing landscape. Spiritual and moral support were unveiled as pillars that fortify the intricate tapestry of success in this industry, emphasizing the importance of a shared ethos and values among network members.

The exploration of recognition and acceptance shed light on the nuanced dynamics of interpersonal relationships, underlining the need for inclusivity and intentional efforts to bridge gaps in diverse network marketing environments. Visualization techniques emerged as a powerful tool for transforming mental images into tangible successes, providing you with a roadmap to navigate the challenges of the industry.

The insights from David Imonitie served as a guiding beacon, emphasizing the principles of belief, conception, and achievement. This chapter provided a framework for translating aspirations into concrete actions, driving you toward success in your network marketing endeavors.

The final chapter, "People Are Capital," resonated deeply, emphasizing the critical role of relationships in the pursuit of wealth and success. It underscored the importance of self-development and maintaining positive relationships not only with others but also with oneself. As you've navigated these concepts, you've not only gained insights into network marketing mastery but also unearthed valuable lessons for personal growth and fulfillment.

As you embark on your journey armed with this blueprint for success, may the principles and wisdom acquired serve as a compass guiding you through the intricate terrain of network marketing. Remember, each chapter has woven a thread in the tapestry of your success, and your path forward is illuminated by the collective wisdom gained from these foundational principles. May your network marketing journey be marked by resilience, growth, and, ultimately, success.

Afterwords

"My Blueprint for Success: A Novice's Guide to Network Marketing Mastery" is truly a treasure trove of knowledge for anyone looking to excel in the world of network marketing. This book takes you on an enlightening journey, unraveling the intricacies of the network marketing business model and shedding light on the various payment plans that can pave the way to success. One of the key highlights of this guide is its emphasis on setting realistic and attainable goals, a crucial factor in steering your network marketing journey toward success.

Moreover, the book places significant importance on the invaluable role of mentors in shaping your path to success. Learning from those who have already walked the path you are embarking upon can provide unparalleled insights and wisdom. The emphasis on cultivating the right attitude is a game-changer, as it underscores the significance of approaching network marketing with a positive and determined mindset.

The visualization techniques and practical exercises presented in the book are truly actionable, offering aspiring network marketers tangible strategies to propel their success. The wisdom shared by David Imonitie adds a layer of depth and authenticity to the insights provided, making it a holistic guide for anyone aspiring to thrive in the dynamic realm of network marketing.

This book doesn't just stop at offering guidance – it serves as a motivational beacon, igniting the flames of determination and perseverance within its readers. It's not just a guide; it's a roadmap that leads you through the twists and turns of network marketing, providing practical advice and motivational insights every step of the way.

"My Blueprint for Success" is indeed an indispensable resource for anyone venturing into network marketing. It's not just a guidebook; it's a companion that stands by you, offering wisdom, motivation, and a clear pathway to success in the ever-evolving industry of network marketing. With its practical advice and comprehensive approach, this book has the power to transform novices into masters of the network marketing domain.

I'm incredibly passionate about the organization I'm a part of, and I can't wait to share more about it with you. This organization offers a revolutionary health and fitness product that has completely transformed my life. It's not just a product; it's a game-changer. Since incorporating it into my daily routine, I've experienced a remarkable improvement in my overall health. The fog that used to cloud my mind has lifted, and I now have a level of clarity and focus that I never thought possible. This newfound mental acuity has ignited a hunger for knowledge within me, and I feel more determined and inspired than ever before. My confidence in my own success has soared.

One of the most incredible benefits of this product is the way it has opened my mind to new possibilities. I find myself absorbing and retaining information at a level I never thought achievable. Life has taken on a whole new dimension, and I'm filled with a sense of vitality and optimism for the future. Not only do I feel rejuvenated on the inside, but I've also noticed a visible difference on the outside. The signs of aging have been reversed at a cellular level, leaving me looking and feeling younger than I have in years. It's truly remarkable how this product has revitalized my cells, allowing them to function with the vigor of a newborn.

I am beyond excited to extend an invitation to you to join me in this incredible journey. By becoming a part of this organization, you'll be entering into a life-changing and paradigm-shifting experience. I can personally guarantee that you'll be welcomed into a supportive environment where your success is the top priority. Our team's uplines are deeply invested in seeing you thrive, and together, we will create a community that fosters growth and achievement.

If you're considering getting involved in network marketing and are seeking a product that has the potential to transform your life, I urge you to follow the link, sign up, and join my team. You won't just be joining an organization; you'll be embarking on a path toward personal and professional fulfillment. As you take this step, know that I am committed to being there for you every step of the way. I'm here to support your growth as a network marketer and to assist in your personal development journey.

I can't wait for you to experience the incredible transformation that this product and organization have brought into my life. Together, we can achieve remarkable success and create positive change in the lives of others. Let's embark on this journey together and make an impact that extends far beyond ourselves.

Applying the Lesson From My Book to a Beginner's Journey

Applying the lessons from my book to your journey in this industry is incredibly beneficial. Start by breaking down the concepts and techniques from the book into manageable chunks (see Appendix). As a beginner, it's important to focus on building a strong foundation of knowledge and skills (see Further Reading). Take the time to understand the fundamental principles outlined in the book and practice applying them in real-world scenarios.

Additionally, seek out opportunities to network with professionals in your upline who can provide guidance and mentorship. This can help reinforce the concepts from the book and provide valuable insights into the practical application of the lessons. Don't be afraid to ask questions and seek feedback from experienced individuals who can offer valuable perspectives.

Furthermore, consider how you can adapt the lessons from this book to your specific interests and career goals within your organization. Whether it's through internships, projects, or further education, look for ways to gain hands-on experience and deepen your understanding of the concepts presented here.

Remember, learning is a continuous journey, so stay curious and open-minded as you apply the lessons from my book to your career in your organization. Embrace challenges as opportunities for growth and continue seeking out resources, such as additional books, workshops, and online courses, to further expand your knowledge and skill set.

By applying the lessons from my book with dedication and enthusiasm, you can set yourself on a rewarding path toward success in the industry. Good luck on your journey, and remember that every step forward is a valuable part of your learning experience!

Further Reading

1. "The Holy Bible King James Version"

2. "As A Man Thinketh" by James Allen

3. "Awaken the Giant Within" by Anthony Robbins

4. "Beyond Wealth" by Alexander Green

5. "Character Still Counts" by James Merritt

6. "Conceive, Believe, Achieve" by David Imonitie

7. "Destiny" by TD Jakes

8. "First Things First" by Stephen R. Covey

9. "How to Win Friends and Influence People" by Dale Carnegie

10. "Hung by the Tongue" by Frances R. Martin

11. "In Search of Black America" by David J Dent

12. "Living the 7 Habits" by Stephen R. Covey

13. "Reconstructing the Dreamland: The Tulsa Riot of 1921" by Alfred Brophy

14. "Rich Dad Poor Dad Cashflow Quadrant" by Robert T. Kiyosaki

15. "Soar" by T.D. Jakes

16. "The Burning: Massacre, Destruction, and the Tulsa Race Riot of 1921" by Tim Madigan

17. "The Eighth Habit" by Stephen R. Covey

18. "7 Habits of Highly Effective People" by Stephen R. Covey

19. "The Magic of Believing" by Claude Bristol

20. "The Power Principle" by Blaine Lee

21. "Think and Grow Rich" by Napoleon Hill

22. "Your Ideal Future" by Benjamin Hardy

Appendix

Key Points

Chapter One

- Setting realistic goals is crucial in network marketing, following the SMART criteria: specific, measurable, achievable, relevant, and time-bound.

- Personal growth and self-improvement are essential for achieving network marketing goals.

- Mentorship and training programs play a vital role in providing knowledge and strategies for success.

- Overcoming personal barriers and developing

a resilient mindset are non-negotiable for success in network marketing.

Chapter Two

- The significance of accessible mentorship in the MLM market

- Overcoming skepticism toward authority figures

- The multifaceted role of the upline in network marketing, extending beyond recruitment and salesmanship

- The importance of personal growth, trust-building, and overcoming past barriers to benefit from mentorship

- The upline's role in nurturing comprehensive personal development and building resilient characters

- Learning from the upline's strategic approaches, including managing networks, stimulating sales, and addressing challenges

- Engaging in dialogue with uplines to understand their strategic motivations and adapting their insights to inform personal strategies

- Keep records and document observations to compile a tangible log of progress.

Chapter Three

- The importance of humility as a key philosophy in business leadership and mentorship

- The role of the upline in fostering humility, teamwork, and personal growth

- Embracing vulnerability and seeking wisdom for genuine progress and fulfillment

- Encouraging open dialogue and setting clear expectations in mentorship relationships

- The multifaceted role of the upline in network marketing, including guiding personal development and nurturing resilient characters.

Chapter Four

- Spiritual support provides inner guidance and purpose beyond monetary gain

- Moral support ensures integrity and ethical conduct in the pursuit of success

- The fortifying framework created by spiritual and moral support

- Finding strength in personal belief systems, particularly through the author's experience with faith

- The role of spirituality and ethics in the journeys of success for network marketers, as shared by the author's uplines.

Chapter Five

- The need for a conscious effort to create an inclusive environment in network marketing

Chapter Seven

David Imonitie's Book: Conceive, Believe, Achieve

Chapter 1: His Story

- *David started out in network marketing with aspirations for a life of affluence and influence.*

- *He faced challenges and obstacles, and his initial attempts at the business did not yield the results he expected.*

- *He experienced a lack of quick results and encountered difficulties in achieving his goals.*

Chapter 2: The Network Marketing Industry

- *David expresses his love for the concept of helping people achieve their goals, regardless of their background.*

- *He emphasizes the importance of going through a process that allows individuals to become the person they want to be.*

- *The emotional, mental, and spiritual breakthrough is crucial to understanding the process.*

Chapter 3: Picture the End Result

- *David emphasizes the importance of beginning with the end in mind and maintaining a clear vision of the desired outcome.*

- *He shares a personal experience of sleeping in his car after giving presentations, highlighting the commitment driven by a clear vision.*

Chapter 4: Have a Mentor or Coach

- *David stresses the importance of humility and recognizing the need for guidance from a mentor or coach.*

- *Having someone to guide and impart knowledge can accelerate progress and help avoid common problems.*

Chapter 5: Live In a Vision Environment

- *Surrounding oneself with reminders of the future life and self creates a vision environment that influences the subconscious mind.*

- *Living in the future environment means creating it now and immersing oneself in experiences that lead to the desired outcome.*

Chapter 6: The Power of Belief

- *Immersing oneself in an environment that aligns with desires can produce corresponding feelings and emotions.*

- *Experiencing and visualizing desires before they happen is key to shaping thoughts and the environment.*

Chapter 7: The Belief System

- *Living in the future while taking action in the present is essential to achieving the desired future.*

- *Crafting a self-portrait and eliminating anything or anyone that doesn't support that self-image is crucial to success.*

Chapter 8: We Become What We Think About

- *Our thoughts shape our personality, character, lifestyle, attitude, and behavior.*

- *Deliberate exposure to experiences that align with the desired self-image can actively shape personal development.*

Chapter 9: How to Build a Network Marketing Organization

- *Understanding that network marketing is a real business where people are the capital is crucial.*

- *The importance of humility, coachability, and teachability in potential recruits is emphasized.*

Chapter 10: Prospecting

- *Effective communication through various modes is essential in prospecting for network marketing opportunities.*

- *Building authentic connections while effectively conveying product value is key to successful prospecting.*

Chapter Eight

- Money is essential for acquiring life's necessities and possesses the ability to help oneself and others.

- Money is received in exchange for labor and can also be used to generate more money through business, investments, and ownership.

- The involvement of human beings is crucial in the process of making money, whether through employment, business, investment, or ownership.

- Good relationships with people are essential for acquiring and maintaining wealth and money.

- The relationship with oneself is equally important, as a damaged self-concept can lead to fears, anxieties, and self-sabotaging behaviors that affect interactions with others and financial success.

- Personal development is crucial for establishing good relationships with people and bringing value to them, which in turn leads to financial transactions and success.

Actionable Items

1. Network Marketing Foundation

- Focus on personal development, effective communication, and financial success.

- Set clear goals and develop a daily routine that aligns with the broader vision for network marketing endeavors.

2. Learning from Your Upline

- Engage in open dialogue with uplines to understand their strategic motivations.

- Keep records and document observations to compile a tangible log of progress.

3. The Power of Humility

- Embrace vulnerability and seek wisdom for genuine progress and fulfillment.

- Foster an atmosphere of inclusivity and address implicit biases to build a cohesive and principled network marketing organization.

4. Spiritual and Moral Support

- Cultivate an environment of spiritual and moral support to contribute to the organization's resilience and vibrancy.

- Implement diversity awareness training and initiatives to promote inclusivity within the organization.

5. Recognition and Acceptance

- Consciously counter implicit biases with intentional inclusiveness.

- Create a welcoming environment by actively engaging with individuals of diverse backgrounds.

6. Visualization Techniques

- Incorporate visualization techniques into daily routines to boost focus, motivation, and performance.

- Practice the "mapping" visualization technique to vividly picture desired outcomes and immerse in the details of success.

7. David Imonitie: Conceive, Believe, and Achieve

Chapter 1: His Story

- *Embrace perseverance and resilience in the face of challenges and unexpected outcomes.*

Chapter 2: The Network Marketing Industry

- *Focus on emotional, mental, and spiritual growth to become the person you aspire to be.*

Chapter 3: Picture the End Result

- *Maintain a clear vision of the desired outcome and commit to achieving it.*

Chapter 4: Have a Mentor or Coach

- *Recognize the value of guidance and mentorship in accelerating personal and professional growth.*

Chapter 5: Live In a Vision Environment

- *Surround yourself with reminders of your future life and immerse yourself in experiences that lead to your desired outcome.*

Chapter 6: The Power of Belief

- *Immerse yourself in an environment that aligns with your desires and visualize your success.*

Chapter 7: The Belief System

- *Take action in the present while living in the future and eliminate anything or anyone that doesn't support your self-image.*

Chapter 8: We Become What We Think About

- *Deliberately expose yourself to experiences that align with your desired self-image to actively shape your personal development.*

Chapter 9: How to Build a Network Marketing Organization

- *Understand that people are the capital in network marketing and value humility, coachability, and teachability in potential recruits.*

Chapter 10: Prospecting

- *Communicate effectively and build authentic connections while effectively conveying product value for successful prospecting.*

8. People Are Capital

- Establish good relationships with people and bring them value.

- Work on personal development to build a healthy self-concept and overcome fears, anxieties, and self-sabotaging behaviors.

- Use money for personal development, as "money helpeth all things."

- Focus on building a foundation of internal abundance and eternal wealth.

About the Author

Floyd Jones Sanders is the Principal and Managing Director at P.A.C.E. Family Services, an agency providing anger parenting, anger management Counseling, and Exchange services in California. Floyd graduated from UC Davis with a degree in Analytic Philosophy and History. He is a professional anger management counselor, certified Domestic Violence therapist, and Life Coach. He is certified in the ABCs of Parenting through Yale University. Floyd has over 25 years of experience in the field of individual counseling, coaching, and family services.

He currently lives in Sacramento, California. If you would like more information about coaching/counseling services or the network marketing company Floyd is a part of, or you are interested in becoming a distributor or customer, see the contact information information below.

www.pacefamilyservices.com

www.floydsanders.lifevantage.com

email: floydj.sanders@outlooklook.com